Wallace & Gromit ™

in

A Grand Day Out ™

Student's Book

Peter Viney and Karen Viney

OXFORD
UNIVERSITY PRESS

OXFORD
UNIVERSITY PRESS

Great Clarendon Street, Oxford OX2 6DP

Oxford University Press is a department of the University of Oxford.
It furthers the University's objective of excellence in research, scholarship,
and education by publishing worldwide in

Oxford New York

Auckland Cape Town Dar es Salaam Hong Kong Karachi
Kuala Lumpur Madrid Melbourne Mexico City Nairobi
New Delhi Shanghai Taipei Toronto

With offices in

Argentina Austria Brazil Chile Czech Republic France Greece
Guatemala Hungary Italy Japan Poland Portugal Singapore
South Korea Switzerland Thailand Turkey Ukraine Vietnam

OXFORD and OXFORD ENGLISH are registered trade marks of
Oxford University Press in the UK and in certain other countries

ISBN-13: 978 0 19 459245 1	Student's Book
ISBN-13: 978 0 19 459246 8	Teacher's Book
ISBN-13: 978 0 19 459247 5	VHS PAL Video Cassette
ISBN-13: 978 0 19 459249 9	VHS SECAM Video Cassette
ISBN-13: 978 0 19 459248 2	VHS NTSC Video Cassette
ISBN-13: 978 0 19 459238 3	DVD

ISBN-10: 0 19 459245 6	Student's Book
ISBN-10: 0 19 459246 4	Teacher's Book
ISBN-10: 0 19 459247 2	VHS PAL Video Cassette
ISBN-10: 0 19 459249 9	VHS SECAM Video Cassette
ISBN-10: 0 19 459248 0	VHS NTSC Video Cassette
ISBN-10: 0 19 459238 3	DVD

Printed in China

ACKNOWLEDGEMENTS

Design by: Stephen Strong

Illustrations by: Bill Kerwin

The publishers would like to thank the following for their co-operation and assistance:
Aardman Animations Ltd.; Pinewood Studios

Adaptor's acknowledgement: The adaptor would like to thank the following
people at Oxford University Press for their commitment and enthusiasm:
Robert Maidment, who produced the ELT adaptation of *A Grand Day Out*;
Martyn Hobbs, who edited the ELT version; and Tim Blakey who edited the
Student's Book

Contents

Meet Wallace and Gromit™

His name is Wallace.
He lives in England.

His name is Gromit.
He's a dog.
He lives with Wallace.

What about you?

My name is

I live in

I live with

Holiday plans

Watching the video

Before you watch

 1 Ask and answer.

What's your favourite holiday?

A camping holiday.

camping holiday

skiing holiday

beach holiday

walking holiday

 Watch all of episode one.

After you watch

2 Tick (✔) the answer.

1 Who's reading a book?		
2 Who's sleeping?		
3 Who's reading a holiday magazine?		
4 Who's making tea?		
5 Who's eating a cracker?		

4

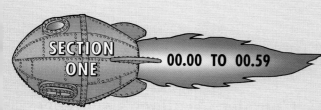

SECTION ONE
00.00 TO 00.59

Before you watch

1   Write answers.

Who's sitting here?

_____

Who's sitting here?

_____

 Watch section one.

After you watch

2   Can you repeat?

cup of tea
hot cup of tea
nice hot cup of tea
a nice hot cup of tea
have a nice hot cup of tea
Let's have a nice hot cup of tea.

cheese
bit of cheese
nice bit of cheese
a nice bit of cheese
And a nice bit of cheese.

SECTION TWO 01.00 TO THE END

Before you watch

1 **Label the picture.**

cracker   cup   plate   saucer   teapot   tray

tray

📺 **Watch section two.**

After you watch

2 **Complete Wallace's sentences.**

No _____ in the fridge!

Let's go to a place with _____.

The Moon's made of _____.

3 **What countries does Wallace say? Tick (✔) the boxes.**

America	
England	
France	
Brazil	
Italy	✔
Japan	
Spain	
Turkey	

Watch episode one again.

While you watch

1 **What can you see in episode one? Tick (✔) the boxes.**

a globe ☐   a table ☐   a lamp ☐   a clock ☐

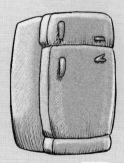

a chair ☐   a newspaper ☐   a fridge ☐

cheese ☐   a cupboard ☐   flowers ☐

a book ☐   a pen ☐   the Moon ☐   stars ☐

 Watch all of episode one again and check.

Practice

1 **Can you remember?**

 Student A:
Look at the picture. Close your book and ask about the tray.

Is there a saucer?

 Student B:
Look at the picture and answer.

Yes, there is.   *No, there isn't.*

2 **Chant**

Chant in two groups.

Group A	Group B
Cheese, please.	No cheese.
Cheese, please.	No cheese.
Please, please!	No cheese.
CHEESE! CHEESE!	NO CHEESE!

3 Let's go ...

 Make conversations.

Let's go to Spain.

OK, let's go.

4 Let's have ...

What's Wallace saying?

a cup of tea

Let's have a cup of tea.

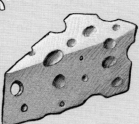
a bit of cheese

some crackers

a holiday

 5 Your class

Make sentences.

Let's go to _____

Let's have _____

9

Narrator Episode one. Holiday plans.

SECTION ONE

Narrator 'Sunny Holidays,' 'Travel Magazine'… Who's going on holiday?
'Skiing', 'Camping Today', 'Picnic Guide'? Who's going on a picnic? Wallace and Gromit!

Wallace We need a holiday, Gromit. Where can we go?
Wake up, Gromit, lad!
Let's have a nice hot cup of tea. Hmm.
And a nice bit of cheese.

SECTION TWO

Narrator Plate, teapot, water and crackers. What's in the fridge?

Wallace No cheese, Gromit. No cheese in the fridge.

Narrator Cups and saucers.

Wallace Gromit, that's it … cheese!
Let's go to a place with cheese! Where can we go?
Cheese holidays in England, France, Italy, Spain …
The Moon's made of cheese!
Let's go to the Moon.

The spaceship

Watching the video

Before you watch

1 **What have you got on your table? Ask and answer.**

Have you got a pencil?

Yes, I have.

No, I haven't.

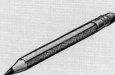

a pencil   a pen

a pencil sharpener   a piece of paper

a book

 Watch all of episode two.

After you watch

2 **Who has got it? Make sentences.**

Wallace has got _____.

Gromit has got _____.

a pencil   a book

a saw

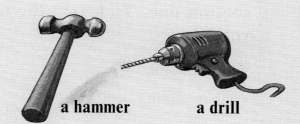

a hammer   a drill

a paintbrush   an umbrella

3 **Ask and answer.**

Has Gromit got a pencil?

Yes, he has.

No, he hasn't.

11

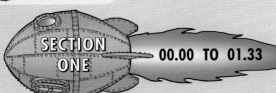

SECTION ONE   00.00 TO 01.33

sniff-sniff

drip-drip

click

squeak-squeak

CREAK

Before you watch

1   **Noises**
Say these noises aloud.
Then match the noises to the pictures.

water dripping   door creaking   mouse sniffing   mice squeaking   light switch clicking

While you watch

2   **You can hear a lot of noises in section one. Tick (✔) the noises you hear.**

water dripping ☐

a mouse sniffing ☐

a door creaking ☐

Wallace coming down the stairs ☐

a clock ticking ☐

mice squeaking ☐

a light switch clicking ☐

Wallace sharpening a pencil ☐

Wallace eating crackers ☐

Wallace drawing on the paper ☐

Wallace saying 'Vrrmmm!' ☐

 Watch section one.

After you watch

3   **Which one can you see?**

   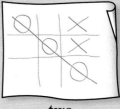

one   two

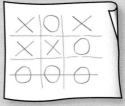

three

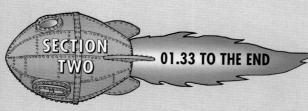

SECTION TWO — 01.33 TO THE END

Before you watch

1 Complete the spaces.

One mouse   Two _____ .

One hole

Three _____ .

 Watch section two.

After you watch

2 Write the sentences on the correct pictures.

◆ Well done, Gromit.
◆ Don't move, Gromit!
◆ Sorry!
◆ Hold on, Gromit!
◆ Be careful!

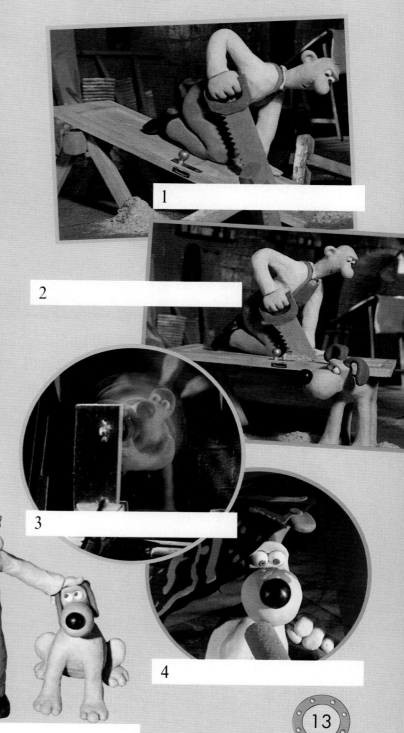

1 _____

2 _____

3 _____

4 _____

5 _____

3 **Complete the sentences.**

drilling sawing reading welding
hammering painting whistling

1 Gromit is _____ a book.

2 Wallace is _____.

3 Wallace is _____.

4 Gromit is _____ a nail.

5 Gromit is _____ a hole.

6 Gromit is _____.

7 Wallace is _____ the spaceship.

4 **Look at the pictures. Ask and answer.**

What's he doing?   He's sawing.

Watch episode two again.

Practice

1 That's a nice colour!

Match the spaceships to the colours.

1 2 3 4 5 6 7 8 9 10

| black | white | grey | red | green | blue | yellow | brown | orange | pink |

Ask and answer about things in the classroom.

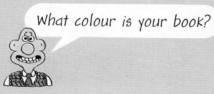 What colour is your book? It's black.

2 Chant

Chant in two groups.

Group A	Group B
Water dripping,	drip drip.
Mouse sniffing,	sniff sniff.
Door creaking,	creak creak.
Mice squeaking,	squeak squeak.
Wallace eating,	crunch crunch.
Hammers beating,	bang bang.
Spaceship flying,	vroom vroom.
Gromit flying	Woah WOAH!

3 Pets

 Find these pets in the picture.

| a cat | a hamster | a dog | a rabbit | a mouse | a bird | a fish |

Match the questions to the answers.

1	Have you got a pet?	A	Squeaker.
2	What is it?	B	White.
3	Has it got a name?	C	Yes, I have.
4	What's its name?	D	A mouse.
5	What colour is it?	E	Yes, it has.

 Ask and answer about your pets.

4 Be careful!

Student A: Give instructions.

stand UP.

Sit down.

Don't move.

Open your *book.*

Close your book.

Be careful!

Smile.

Student B: Follow the instructions.

Transcript

Narrator Episode two. The spaceship.

SECTION ONE

Narrator It's dark in the cellar. A mouse!
Who's that? It's Wallace.
He's coming down the stairs.
Paper. A pencil. What are you drawing, Wallace?
Noughts and crosses.
A spaceship! That's Gromit.
And that's Wallace.

Wallace Vrrmm!

SECTION TWO

Narrator Be careful!

Wallace Oh!

Narrator Too late!

Wallace Hmm …

Narrator What's Gromit doing?
He's reading a book.

Narrator Don't move, Gromit!
It's hard work! One hole …
two holes … three holes.
Wallace has got a hammer.
Gromit has got a drill.
Hold on, Gromit! Be careful!
Wallace is painting the spaceship …
orange.

Wallace Sorry!

Narrator That's a nice colour. The mice like it.
Well done, Gromit. It's amazing!

Episode 3

Blast off!

Watching the video

Before you watch

1 **Countdown**
Look at ten (10). Put the numbers in words.

10 **9** **8** **7** **6** **5** **4** **3** **2** **1** **BLAST OFF**

ten

| three | seven | two | five | one | eight | four | six | nine |

🚀 **Count from ten to one.**   🚀 **Count from one to ten.**

📺 **Watch all of episode three.**

After you watch

2 **Label the pictures.**

controls   ladder   suitcase
clock   match   fuse   brake

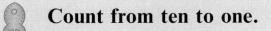

1

4

3

6

2

5

7

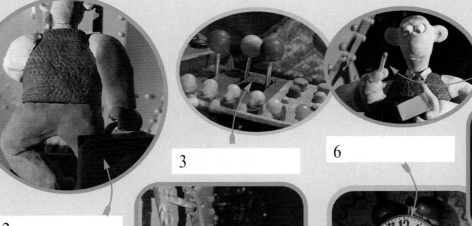

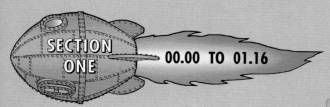

SECTION ONE 00.00 TO 01.16

Before you watch

1 **Complete the spaces.**

into	up	down

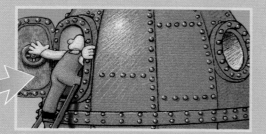

_____ the stairs. _____ the ladder.

_____ the spaceship.

_____ the ladder. _____ the ladder again.

 Watch section one.

After you watch

2 **Match the sentences to the pictures.**

1 Light the fuse.
2 Wallace has got his suitcase.
3 Gromit's at the controls.
4 Strike a match.

SECTION TWO — 01.16 TO THE END

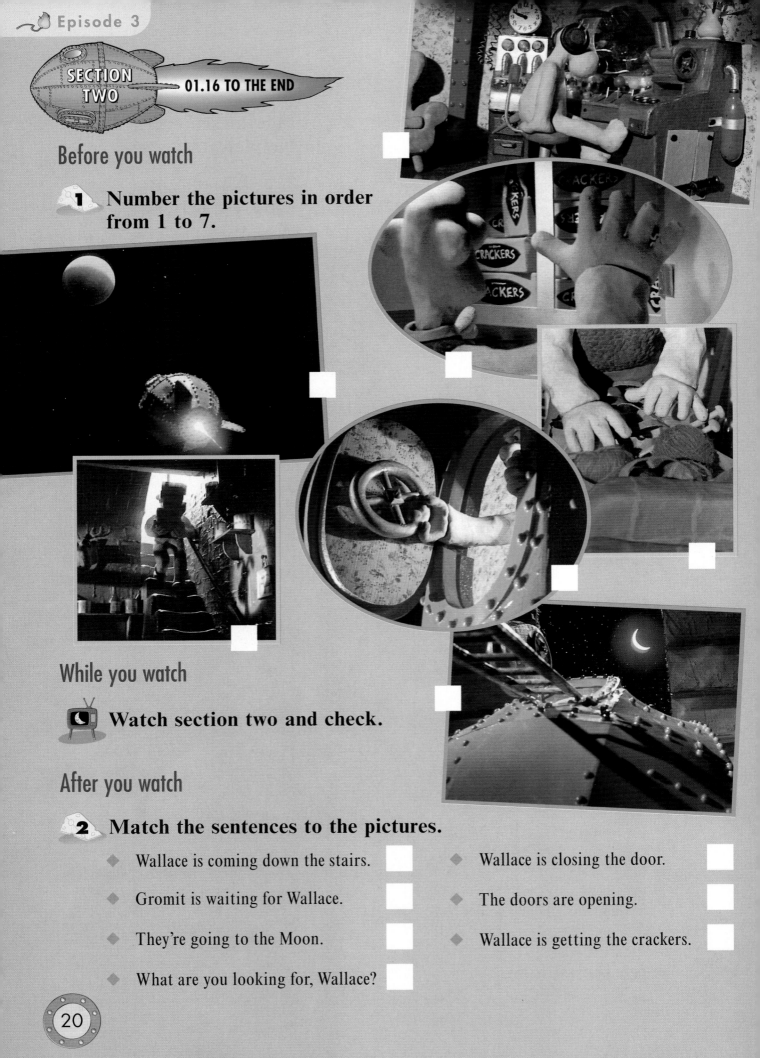

Before you watch

1 Number the pictures in order from 1 to 7.

While you watch

📺 Watch section two and check.

After you watch

2 Match the sentences to the pictures.

◆ Wallace is coming down the stairs.

◆ Gromit is waiting for Wallace.

◆ They're going to the Moon.

◆ What are you looking for, Wallace?

◆ Wallace is closing the door.

◆ The doors are opening.

◆ Wallace is getting the crackers.

We're ready _____.

Before you watch again

3 **Complete Wallace's sentences.**

Let me _____.

Sixty seconds to _____.

We haven't _____ the crackers.

Wait for _____, Gromit.

While you watch

4 **Watch and check.**

 Watch episode three again.

21

Practice

1 Numbers

Put the numbers on the clock.

fifty	forty	thirty	twenty	sixty
ten	fifteen	fifty-five	thirty-five	
	twenty-five	forty-five		

2 Say these numbers aloud.

60... 59... 58... 57... 46... 45...

34... 33... 22... 21... 20...

3 Find the numbers.

1	2	3	4	5	6	7	8	9
10	20	30	40	50	60			

a	t	w	e	n	t	y	f
f	h	s	i	x	t	y	o
i	r	e	i	g	h	t	r
f	i	v	e	h	r	o	t
t	f	e	s	t	e	n	y
y	o	n	i	n	e	e	s
q	u	a	x	t	w	o	p
m	r	t	h	i	r	t	y

22

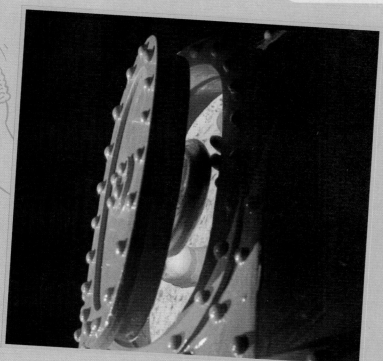

4 Chant

Say aloud.

One, two, three, four.
Up the ladder, in the door.
Five, six, seven, eight.
Hurry up, Wallace. Don't be late.
Down the ladder. Strike a match.
Up the ladder, close the hatch.

5 How many?

Ask and answer.

How many pink sunglasses are there?

Two.

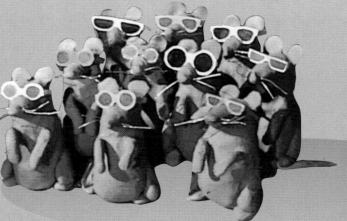

How many mice are there?
How many yellow sunglasses are there?
How many white sunglasses are there?
How many pink sunglasses are there?
How many blue sunglasses are there?
How many green sunglasses are there?

How many tins of paint are there?
How many shelves are there?
How many tins are on the bottom shelf?
How many tins are on the top shelf?

23

Transcript

Narrator Episode three. Blast off!

SECTION ONE

Narrator Gromit's at the controls.
Wallace has got his suitcase.
Up the ladder. Into the
spaceship.

Wallace Let me see. Oooh.
We're ready now. Oh. Uh, ow.

Narrator Down the ladder.
Ah! The fuse. Strike a match.
Light the fuse.
And up the ladder again.

SECTION TWO

Wallace Sixty seconds to blast off.

Narrator Fifty-nine ... fifty-eight ... fifty-seven ...

Wallace Oh. Open the doors.
Ooh. Mmm.

Narrator What are you looking for, Wallace?

Wallace No crackers, Gromit! We haven't got
the crackers!
Wait for me, Gromit!

Narrator Ten ... nine ... eight ... Hurry up,
Wallace! Five ... four ... three ...
two ... one ...

Wallace Uh?

Narrator The brake!
Blast off! They're going to the Moon.

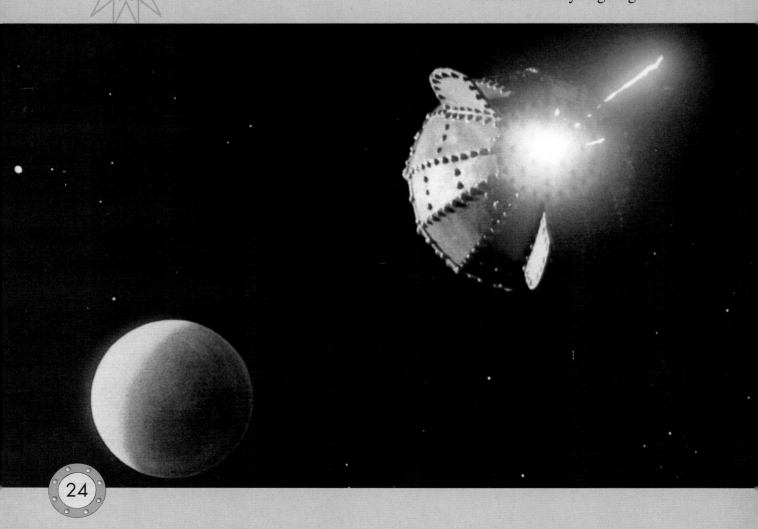

A perfect landing

Watching the video

Before you watch

1 Ask and answer.

Do you like playing cards?

Yes, I do. *No, I don't.*

playing cards

playing football

reading

picnics

cheese

toast

Watch all of episode four.

After you watch

2 Tick (✔) the correct sentences.

You can play football on the Moon. ☐

You can't play football on the Moon. ☐

The toast is hot. ☐

The toast isn't hot. ☐

Wallace likes picnics. ☐

Wallace doesn't like picnics. ☐

The Moon is made of cheese. ☐

The Moon isn't made of cheese. ☐

25

SECTION ONE   00.00 TO 02.04

Before you watch

1 Gromit is building a house of cards. Number the pictures in order from 1 to 7.

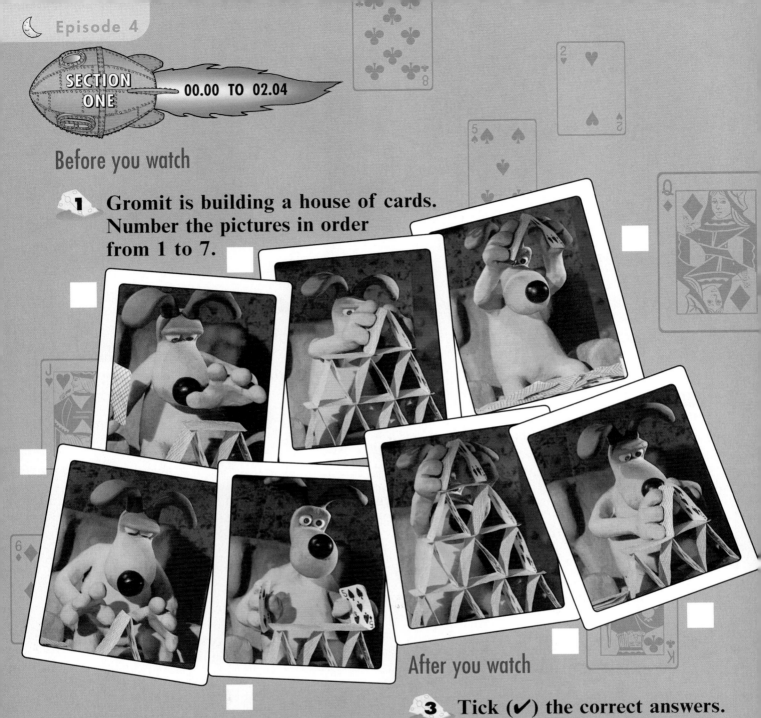

After you watch

2 How many cards are there in the house of cards?

Count the cards in each picture.

Picture number	1	2	3	4	5	6	7
How many cards?							

 Watch section one.

3 Tick (✔) the correct answers.

Questions	Answers
1 Is it a long way to the Moon?	Yes, it is.
	No, it isn't.
2 Has Gromit got some cards?	Yes, he has.
	No, he hasn't.
3 Is Gromit bored?	Yes, he is.
	No, he isn't.
4 Has Gromit got a camera?	Yes, he has.
	No, he hasn't.
5 Is the toast hot?	Yes, it is.
	No, it isn't.

SECTION TWO — 02.04 TO THE END

Before you watch

1 **Label the picture.**

bag Thermos flask basket cup saucer
tablecloth sugar apple cheese

While you watch

2 **Can you remember?**
What has Gromit got in his bag?

 Watch section two and check.

After you watch

3 **Write the sentences on the correct pictures.**

◆ You try it.
◆ I don't know, lad.
◆ What kind is it?

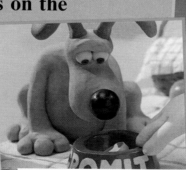

4 **Say the cheese names aloud.**

Wens - ley - dale   Stil - ton
Ched - dar   Gor - gon - zo - la

Do you know more cheese names?

27

Watch episode four again.

After you watch

1 What's happening in the pictures?

e.g.
cut the cheese
Wallace is cutting the cheese.

take a photo
walk on the moon
drink tea
eat cheese
read the newspaper
eat toast
cut the cheese
sniff the cheese
build a house of cards

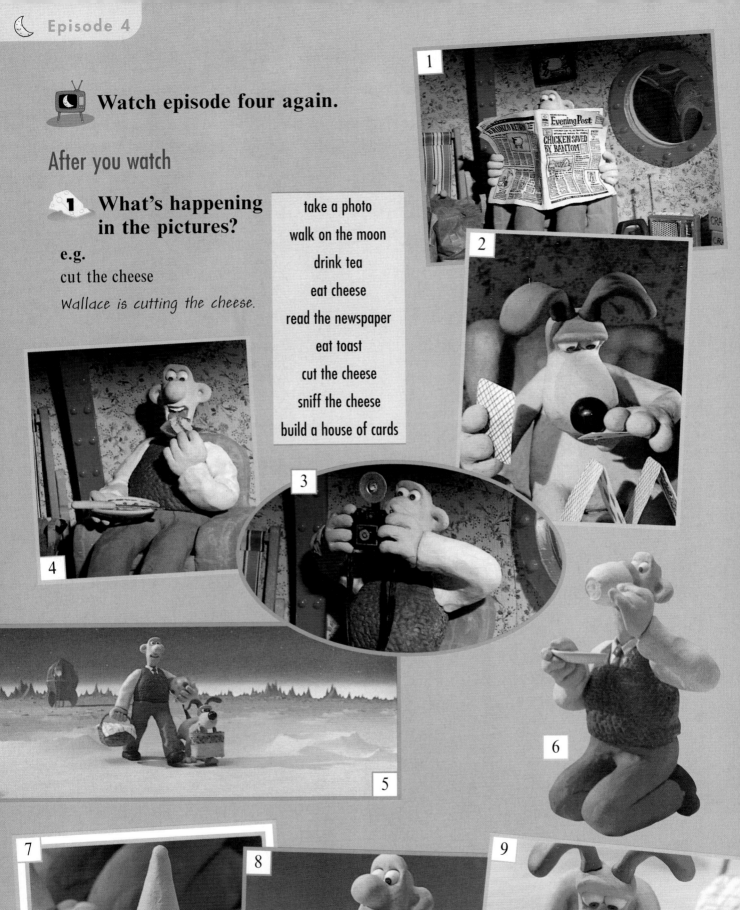

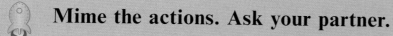

Practice

1 **Mime game**

Mime the actions. Ask your partner.

Actions

taking a photo
building a house of cards
reading a newspaper
eating a cracker
cutting cheese
drinking tea
opening a door
closing a door
waiting for someone
looking for your pen

What am I doing?

You're taking a photo.

I don't know.

2 **Chant**

Say aloud.

I like apples.
I like cheese.
I like honey,
from the bees.
I like reading,
but I like most,
eating honey,
on my toast.

HONEY

3 Spelling

Tick (✔) the correct spelling.

nife		knife		nyfe		knif	
toast		tost		towst		toost	
borred		bawrd		bored		bord	
reddy		readdy		redi		ready	
braek		brak		brake		breke	
happening		hapenning		happenin		hapanning	
reeding		readding		reding		reading	
walkin		warking		walking		walcing	

4 Opposites

Match the opposites.

up	cold
quickly	out
hot	off
on	slowly
in	down

5 Ask your partner to do these things.

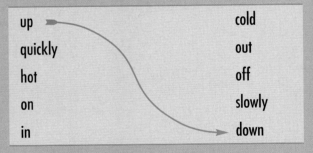

stand **UP** quickly.

Sit down slowly.

stand **UP** slowly.

Sit down quickly.

Walk slowly.

Walk quickly.

Transcript

Narrator	Episode four. A perfect landing.

SECTION ONE

Narrator	It's a long way to the Moon. Gromit's got some playing cards. Wallace is reading the newspaper. Are you bored, Wallace?
Wallace	That's a nice photo. Huh?
Narrator	What's happening? It's toast!
Wallace	Mm. That's hot.
Narrator	What's happening now?
Wallace	Ooh!
Narrator	It's the Moon!
Wallace	Huh? Me? OK. Are you ready for landing? Slowly now. That's it. Slowly. Brake on! Oh dear. Sorry!
Narrator	A perfect landing.

SECTION TWO

Narrator	They're walking on the Moon! You can't play football here, Wallace.
Wallace	I like picnics, Gromit. Hmm. Plate, knife, cracker and cheese. Mm. What kind is it? You try it. Wensleydale? Stilton? Mmm, I don't know, lad. What kind of cheese is it, Gromit? Let's try another place.
Narrator	What's that?

Episode 5

The Moon machine

Watching the video

Before you watch

1 **What can you buy?**

CHOCOLATE   COLD DRINKS

TRAIN TICKETS

What can you buy from slot machines in your town?

Can you buy cold drinks?

 Yes, I can.   No, I can't.

📺 **Watch all of episode five.**

After you watch

2 **What can the Moon machine do?**

Make sentences about the pictures with words from the box.

e.g.
It can see.

write   move   ski   see   read

Ask and answer.

Can it see?

Yes, it can.

32

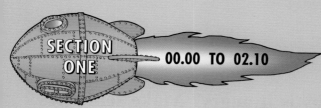

SECTION ONE 00.00 TO 02.10

Before you watch

1 Label the picture.

drawer	control	eye	wheel
antenna	hand	arm	slot

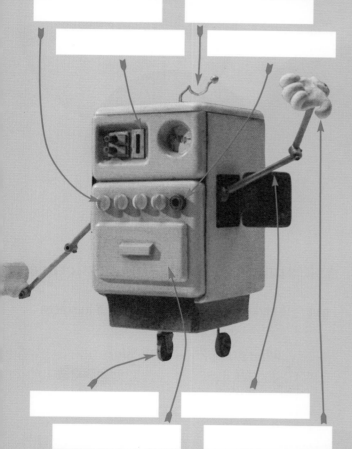

2 Answer the questions.

How many controls has it got?

It's got four controls.

How many wheels has it got?

How many hands has it got?

How many eyes has it got?

 Watch section one.

After you watch

3 Match the sentences to the pictures.

1 And the rest.
2 Open the drawer.
3 Wallace's cup.
4 Money in the slot.
5 It's got a telescope.

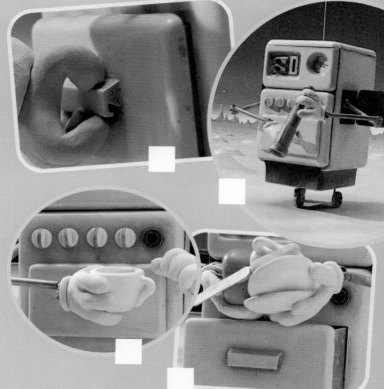

4 Tick (✔) the correct answers.

Questions	Answers	
1 Is it broken?	Yes, it is.	
	No, it isn't.	
2 Is it alive?	Yes, it is.	
	No, it isn't.	
3 Has it got a telescope?	Yes, it has.	
	No, it hasn't.	
4 Can it see?	Yes, it can.	
	No, it can't.	

SECTION TWO 02.10 TO THE END

Before you watch

1 Match the sentences to the pictures.

1 It's angry.
2 It's hurt.
3 It's surprised.

 Watch section two.

 34

After you watch

2 Why is it angry? Make sentences.

e.g.
It's angry about the oil leak.

3 Ask and answer about the pictures.

| glue | a parking ticket | a notebook | a truncheon |

 What's that?

It's glue.

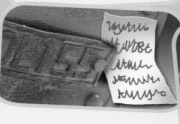

4 At the end, what has the machine got in the drawer?

Can you remember? Make a list.

5 Ask and answer.

Has it got a Thermos flask?

Yes, it has.

I don't know.

No, it hasn't.

 Watch episode five again and check.

 35

Practice

1 Can you do it?

Can you count from one to ten in English?

Yes, I can.

No, I can't.

OK. Count from one to ten.

One, two, three ...

Ask your partner.

1 Can you count from one to ten in English?
2 Can you spell your name in English?
3 Can you draw the Moon machine?
4 Can you draw the spaceship?
5 Can you stand up slowly?
6 Can you write your name quickly?

2 Chant

Say aloud

Put the money in the slot,
Open the drawer.
Now what have you got?
Have you got a chocolate bar?
Have you got a nice blue star?
Have you got a yellow ball?
Oh, dear, there's nothing at all!

3 Match the words to the pictures.

That's better.
Ouch!
Are you hurt?
Gromit can ski.
Be careful, Gromit!

4 Word chain

The last letter in the first word
is the first letter in the next word.

picnic   clock   knife   eye

Can you make a word chain from these words?
Begin: *antenna*   *arm*

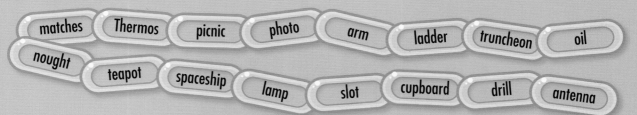

matches   Thermos   picnic   photo   arm   ladder   truncheon   oil
nought   teapot   spaceship   lamp   slot   cupboard   drill   antenna

5 Find the different word.

book	plate	truncheon	apple	yellow	glue
notebook	cup	hammer	orange	green	cracker
magazine	saucer	drill	cheese	blue	toast
newspaper	knife	saw	banana	hot	chocolate

Transcript

Narrator Episode five. The Moon machine.

SECTION ONE

Wallace Mm. A slot machine. Hmm.

Narrator Money in the slot. Open the drawer.

Wallace Where's my chocolate? Oh. That's typical. Tut. The machine's broken. Come on, Gromit.

Narrator Is it broken?
No, it isn't. It's alive!
It's got a telescope!
Ah! The picnic!
Wallace's cup … and saucer.
And the rest!
'Ski Tours'. A skiing holiday.
Aah! In the drawer.

SECTION TWO

Narrator The cheese.
What's that? It's glue.
That's better.
The spaceship! Turn right.
Ouch!
It's got a notebook and a pencil.
The spaceship's got a parking ticket!
And an oil leak.
Uh oh. It's Wallace.
He's eating cheese.
Oh, dear. The Moon machine's got a truncheon.

Back to the Earth

Watching the video

Before you watch

After you watch

1 **What do you want for your birthday?**

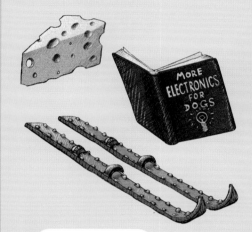

I want cheese.

I want a book.

I want skis.

He wants cheese.
He wants a book.
He wants skis.

 What do you want?

 Watch episode six.

2 **Complete the sentences.**

scared   happy   tired   sad   hurt   angry

Gromit is _____.

Wallace is _____.

Wallace is _____.

The machine is _____.

The machine is _____.

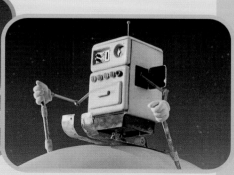

The machine is _____.

39

SECTION ONE 00.00 TO 00.51

Before you watch

1 **Match the sentences with the pictures.**

1 What can you see?
2 More money in the slot.
3 What's wrong, Gromit?
4 I've got the basket.
5 Are you tired, Gromit?
6 The money's run out.

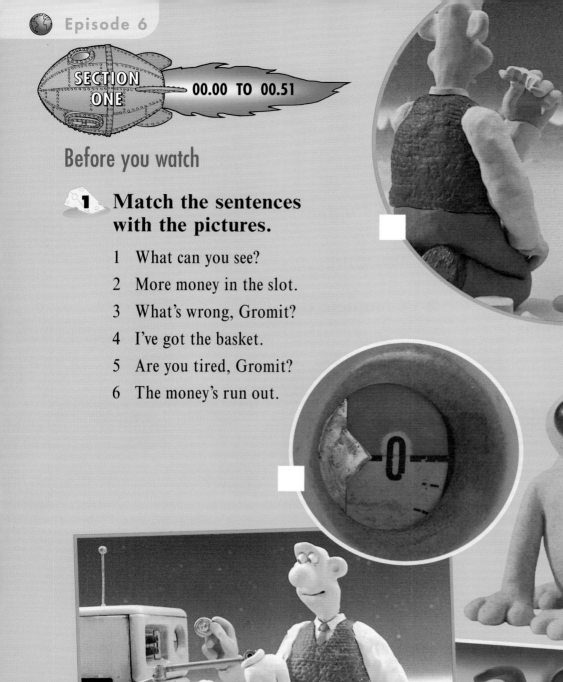

While you watch

Watch section one and check.

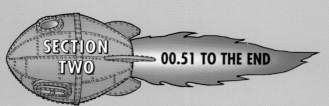

SECTION TWO — 00.51 TO THE END

Before you watch

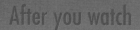

1 Match the words.

Watch section two.

| climb | open | strike | wave | set | read | eat |

| a match | a newspaper | goodbye | the controls |
| cheese | a ladder | a tin |

After you watch

2 Choose the correct words.

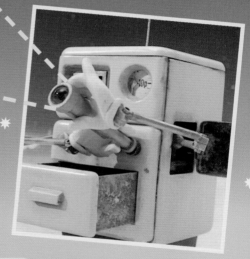

It likes (skiing / skis), but it (don't / can't) ski on the Moon.

It (hasn't / haven't) got any skis. It wants to go to the Earth,

because it (can / can't) ski on the Earth.

It (has / have) got skis now.
It can (ski / skiing) on the
Moon. It's (sad / happy).

3 **Cover the words. Tell the story. Then look at the words.**

It wants to go with Wallace and Gromit.

It can't climb the ladder.

It's got a tin-opener.

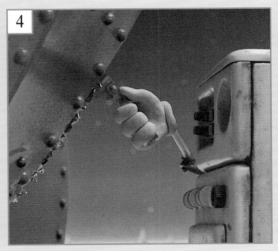

It's opening the spaceship.

It's going inside.

It's dark inside. It can't see.

That's fuel!

Don't strike a match!

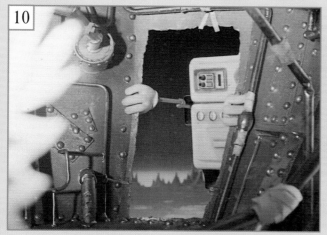

Bang!

Blast off!

The spaceship is going back to the Earth.

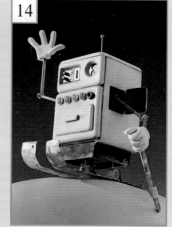

 Watch section two again.

In a later lesson

 Watch all of 'A Grand Day Out'.
Don't stop the video.

Practice

1 Going home

Ask and answer.

What's Wallace doing?
Who is he waving to?

What's Wallace doing?
What is he eating?
Does he like the Moon cheese?

Who is setting the controls?
Where are they going?

2 Don't do it!

Say aloud.

Student A	Student B
Strike a match!	*Don't strike a match!*
Climb the ladder!	No, _____.
	_____.
Close the door!	No, _____.
	_____.
Light the fuse!	No, _____.
	_____.
Wave goodbye!	No, _____.
	_____.

3 Sounds

Say the words aloud. Find the word with the different sound.

see	me	pen	cheese
got	go	slot	hot
fuse	fuel	glue	run
like	strike	climb	ski
danger	wave	back	play
happy	sad	match	want

Transcript

Narrator	Episode six. Back to the Earth.

SECTION ONE

Narrator	Are you tired, Gromit? What can you see?
Wallace	It's OK. Hmm.
Narrator	The money's run out. Phew!
Wallace	Camembert? Oh. Owww! Huh ...Oh. Oh. Mm, hm.
Narrator	More money in the slot. What's wrong, Gromit?
Wallace	Let's go back to the Earth. I've got the basket.

SECTION TWO

Narrator	The spaceship. And the Earth! It can ski on the Earth. It wants to go with you!
Wallace	Oh! My cheese!
Narrator	It can't climb the ladder.
Wallace	It's coming after us! Ten seconds to blast off!
Narrator	A tin-opener!
Wallace	Hurry up ... Seven seconds to blast off ...
Narrator	It's going inside. That's fuel! Don't strike a match!
Wallace	Oh, the fuse! What about the fuse?
Narrator	Danger! Fuel! Blast off!
Narrator	What can you see? It's the Moon machine. It's sad. It's got skis. And it's skiing! The Moon machine's waving goodbye. It's happy now. It can ski on the Moon.
Wallace	Set the controls for sixty-two West Wallaby Street. Mmm. I like this Moon cheese, Gromit.

45

Picture dictionary

antenna

apple

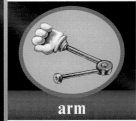
arm

bag

basket

brake

cheese

chocolate

controls

crackers

cross (x)

cup

cupboard

door

drill

the Earth

hand

mouse

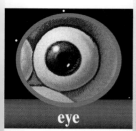

eye

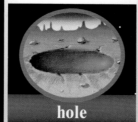

hole

newspaper

fridge

knife

nought (0)

fuel

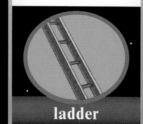

ladder

oil

fuse

matches

paint

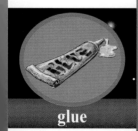

glue

money

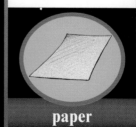

paper

hammer

the Moon

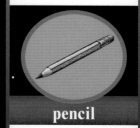

pencil

photo

picnic

plate

playing cards

saucer

shelf / shelves

skis

slot machine

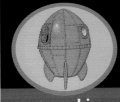

spaceship

suitcase

sunglasses

teapot

telescope

Thermos flask

tin

tin-opener

toast

tray

truncheon

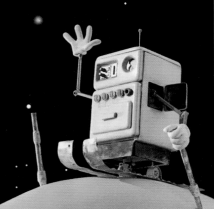